FLOATING
AND
SINKING

Ed Catherall

Science is Fun

Clay Play
Floating and Sinking
Growing Plants
Light and Dark
Our Pets
Sand Play

First published in 1985 by
Wayland (Publishers) Ltd
49 Lansdowne Place, Hove
East Sussex BN3 1HF, England

ISBN 0 85078 506 5

Phototypeset by
Kalligraphics Ltd, Redhill, Surrey
Printed in Italy by
G. Canale & C.S.p.A., Turin
Bound in the U.K. by
The Pitman Press, Bath

CONTENTS

Sinking

Collect some objects you think will **sink** in water.

Half fill a large bowl with water.
Try each object in the water.
Does each object sink?

What are your sinking objects made of?
Which objects are solid?

Why do you think the objects sank?

Sinking like a stone

Make a collection of different stones.
Place a stone in water.
Does the stone sink?
Do all of your stones sink?
Do the stones go straight down when they sink?

How does a coin sink?

Floating

Collect some objects you think will **float.**
Place each object on the surface of the water.
Does the object float?

How much of each floating object is under water?
What are your floating objects made of?
Which objects are hollow?

Can you make your floating objects sink?
What do you think makes things float?

That floating feeling

Push a floating object under the water.
Let go of the object under water.
What happens?

Float a table tennis ball on water.
Push the ball under the water.
What can you feel?
What happens when you let go of the ball.
Which other objects float like your ball?

Floating and sinking

Tear a paper towel into pieces.
Place a piece of paper on the surface of the water.
Does the paper float?
Wait.
What happens to the paper?

Push the paper under the water.
Let go of the paper under the water.
What happens?
Does the paper still float?

Looking at sponges

Put a dry sponge on the surface of the water.
Does the sponge float?
Wait.
What happens to the sponge?

Squeeze the sponge under water.
Do bubbles come from the sponge?
Let go of the squeezed sponge under water.
Does the sponge still float?

What are sponges used for?

An empty bottle

Find a clean, empty, plastic bottle.
Does this bottle float?

Push the bottle under the water.
Do bubbles of air leave the bottle?
What was in your 'empty' bottle?
Where do the air bubbles go?
What goes into the bottle?

Make sure that all the air is out of the bottle.
Does the bottle still float?

10

A full bottle

Fill a plastic bottle with water.
Does this full bottle sink?

Can you pour water out of
the bottle when it is under the water?
What do you have to do to pour out the water?
What goes into the bottle as the water comes out?

Make sure that all the water is out of the bottle.
Does the bottle still sink?

Raising wrecks

Find a clean, empty, plastic bottle.
Push the bottle under the water until it sinks.
Put one end of some plastic tubing into the bottle.
Put the other end of the tubing into your mouth.

Slowly blow air into the bottle.
What happens to the water in the bottle?
Does the bottle float when it is full of air?

This is how shipwrecks are raised from the sea bed.

A submarine

Find an empty plastic bottle with a cap.
Does this empty bottle float?
Fill the bottle with water.
Does the full bottle sink?

Pour out some of the water and replace the cap.
Look at how the bottle floats.
Put more water into the bottle until
the bottle floats just below the surface.
Your bottle is now floating just like a submarine.

A balloon in water

Half fill a bucket with water.
Blow up a balloon to about half its full size.
Tie the neck of the balloon to keep in the air.

Push the balloon under the water.
What do you feel?
Let out the air from the balloon under water.
What happens?

Do you wear arm bands when you swim?

Changing water levels

Half fill a bucket with water.
Mark the water level on the side of the bucket.

Blow up a balloon.
Hold the neck of the balloon to keep in the air.
Push the balloon under the water.
What happens to the water level in the bucket?

Put more air into the balloon.
Push the balloon under the water again.
What happens to the water level now?

A floating can

Put a large empty can into a bucket of water.
Put a disc of clay in the can.
Does the can float?

Mark the water level on the side of the bowl and
on the side of the can.
Keep loading the can with discs.
What happens to the water level on the bowl?
What happens to the water level on the can?
What makes the water level change?
How can you tell if a ship is loaded or empty?

Making clay boats

Find a ball of soft clay.
Does this ball of clay sink?

Make the clay into a boat with thick sides.
Does your boat float?
Make the sides of your boat thinner.
Does this boat float?

Make different shapes and sizes of clay boats.
Which boat floats the best?

Making foil boats

Use cooking foil to make boats.
Fold over the corners of your boats.
This will stop water flowing in.
Do your metal boats float?
What happens if you push your boat under water?

Use polystyrene trays as boats.
Push the tray under the water.
What happens?
Load your tray with clay.
What happens?

Loading boats

Float a polystyrene tray on water.
Load your tray with small nails.
How many nails can you put on
your tray before it sinks?
Where did you have to put the nails on the tray?

Put the nails on one corner of the tray.
What happens?

Making a bubble can

Find a can of clear soup.
Ask an adult to make a hole in the middle of the top
and in the base of the can as well.
Make sure there are no sharp edges.
Drain out the soup and wash out the can.

Push the can under the water.
What comes out of the can?
What goes into the can?

A magic water can

Push your bubble can under the water.
Lift the can out of the water.
What happens?
Press your finger over the hole in the top.
Does water still stream out of the bottom?
Take your finger away from the hole for an instant.
What happens?

Your finger stops air from getting into the can.
This controls the flow of the water.

A sinking can

Put your bubble can on the surface of the water.
Make sure that one hole is under water.
Watch your can sink.

Drain the water out of the can.
Cover the top hole with clay.
Put your can on the surface of the water.
Make sure that the hole without the clay
is under the water.
Does this can sink?

Water and sinking

Ask an adult to make a hole
in the bottom of a large, empty can.
Place the can in a bucket of water.
Does your can sink?

Empty the water out of the can.
Push the can deep into the water until
the water nearly comes over the top of the can.
What can you feel?
Watch how the water comes into the hole in the can.

GLOSSARY

Disc   A flat, round shape.

Foil   A very thin metal sheet.

Hollow   An object is hollow if it has empty space inside it.

Polystyrene   A hard, white plastic foam.

Shipwreck   A ship that has been destroyed or sunk while at sea.

Solid   An object is solid if it does not have any empty space inside it.

Sponge   Something thick and soft, with lots of holes in it. Sponges soak up water.

Surface   The top or outside of something.

Tubing   A long, thin and hollow piece of plastic, glass, rubber or metal, which water can be pumped through.

INDEX